Wild Weather

BIG FREEZE

Heinemann
LIBRARY

Catherine Chambers

www.heinemann.co.uk/library
Visit our website to find out more information about **Heinemann Library** books.

To order:
 Phone ++44 (0)1865 888066
 Send a fax to ++44 (0)1865 314091
 Visit the Heinemann Bookshop at www.heinemann.co.uk/library to browse our catalogue and order online.

First published in Great Britain by Heinemann Library, Halley Court, Jordan Hill, Oxford
OX2 8EJ, a division of Reed Educational and Professional Publishing Ltd. Heinemann
is a registered trademark of Reed Educational & Professional Publishing Ltd.

OXFORD MELBOURNE AUCKLAND JOHANNESBURG BLANTYRE
GABORONE IBADAN PORTSMOUTH NH (USA) CHICAGO

Designed by Visual Image
Illustration by Paul Bale
Originated by Ambassador Litho Ltd.
Printed and bound in South China.

ISBN 0 431 15068 0

06 05 04 03 02
10 9 8 7 6 5 4 3 2 1

British Library Cataloguing in Publication Data

Chambers, Catherine
Big Freeze. – (Wild Weather)
1. Big Freeze – (Meteorology) – Juvenile literature
I. Title
551.5'253

Acknowledgements

The Publishers would like to thank the following for permission to reproduce photographs: Ardea p19, Associated Press
p26, Bryan and Cherry Alexander p27, Corbis pp5, 11, 16, 17, 22, 24, 29, Imagebank p15, Photodisc pp4, 12, 13, 14, 28,
Reaters pp20, 23, Robert Harding Picture Library p6, Stone pp7, 18, 21, 25, Telegraph Colour Library p9.

Cover photograph reproduced with permission of Photodisc.

Every effort has been made to contact copyright holders of any material reproduced in this book.
Any omissions will be rectified in subsequent printings if notice is given to the Publisher.

Any words appearing in the text in bold, **like this**, are explained in the Glossary.

Contents

What is a big freeze?

Some places on Earth are cold all year round. Others are warm all year round, but most places are cool in winter and warm in the summer.

Winter is usually about the same temperature
every year. Sometimes it gets much colder than
normal, even for winter. Rivers, lakes and the
ground may **freeze**. This is called a big freeze.

Where do big freezes happen?

The areas around the **North and South Poles** are cold all the time. Winter weather is normal there so it is not called a big **freeze**.

Florida in the USA is usually warm. When it
suddenly gets cold there, people, plants and
animals may not be ready. They can be harmed
by the cold. This is a big freeze.

What makes it so cold?

At the **North and South Poles**, the Sun's rays spread over a wider area. This makes the Sun's warmth weaker. In winter, these places **tilt** away from the Sun. The air and ground get really cold.

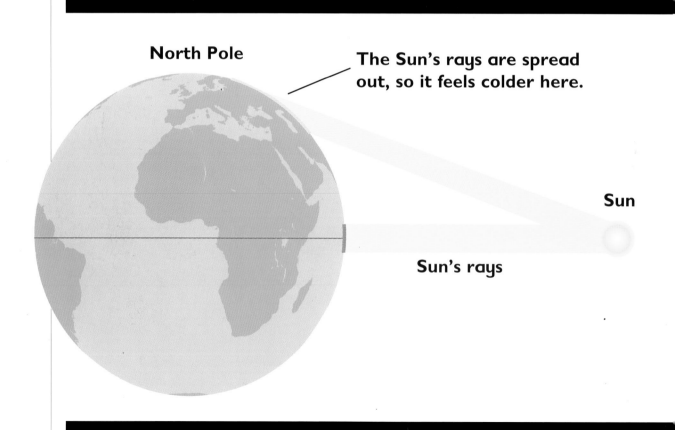

North Pole

The Sun's rays are spread out, so it feels colder here.

Sun

Sun's rays

Days are shorter during the winter so the Sun has less time to warm the Earth. Any heat in the ground rises high above the Earth when there are no clouds to stop it.

Why do big freezes happen?

The Earth is **surrounded** by moving masses of air. Some are warm and some are cold. A big **freeze** happens when a **mass** of cold air stays in one place for a long time.

These masses of cold air often come from around the **North and South Poles**, where it is cold all year round. Strong winds push the cold air to other places, bringing them a big freeze.

What are big freezes like?

In a big **freeze**, the weather is even colder than normal winter weather. It is too cold for people to be outside for very long. They stay inside their heated houses.

Ice covers pavements and roads. People and **vehicles** slip and slide on it. Sometimes ice on roads is **invisible**. It is called **black ice** and is very dangerous.

Harmful freezes

It can be hard to travel in a big **freeze**. Ice can make roads slippery. Water freezes around boats so that they cannot move.

Water freezes inside water pipes. The water **expands** when it freezes. It cracks the pipes. So water gushes out when the big freeze **thaws**. Houses and roads can be flooded.

Big freeze in Outer Mongolia

This is the country of Outer Mongolia. It lies in the middle of the **continent** called Asia. Warm, moist air from the sea cannot reach the middle of the continent

Most people in the country of Outer Mongolia are farmers. In one big **freeze** many cows and sheep died. They died because there was nothing to eat – all the grass was frozen.

Preparing for the big freeze

Some people and shops stock up with food before a big **freeze** comes. They will not have to go outside to go shopping. Hospitals and chemists order plenty of extra medicines.

A big freeze can kill food **crops**. So farmers cover ground crops with **fleece**, foam or glass. They use heaters and wind machines to blow warm air on to fruit trees.

Coping with big freezes

When it is very cold, it is important to dress warmly. Wearing several layers of clothing under your coat will help keep you warm. Mittens, hats and boots are important too.

It is best to stay inside during a big **freeze**.
Getting enough to eat helps your body. Hot
food and drinks are a tasty way to stay warm!

Big freeze in a hot country

India and Bangladesh are normally very hot countries. People's clothes help them to keep cool in the hot weather. Their houses are not built to keep them warm.

In 2001 the weather in these countries was much colder than usual. Many people died because their clothes and houses could not protect them from the **freezing** weather.

Animals and plants in the big freeze

People who live in the Himalayan Mountains keep animals called yaks. Yaks are able to keep warm in the big **freezes** that can happen in the mountains.

If big freezes come too early in the year, they
can damage **crops**. Frost makes plants freeze
and can stop them from growing. These
strawberry plants are covered in ice.

To the rescue!

Cities in warm parts of the world may not have enough snowploughs and salt trucks to cope with a big **freeze**. They may have to borrow trucks from colder places.

Siberia in Russia is very cold in winter. In 2001 it
was even colder than usual. Ice blocked the flow
of the River Lena. Planes dropped bombs on the
thick ice to stop the river from flooding.

Adapting to the big freeze

Most people in this country live in homes with central heating or fires. When a big **freeze** comes they can make their homes warmer.

In many cities there are people without homes.
They sleep outside on the street. For homeless
people, a big freeze can be dangerous. It is
important that they find food and **shelter**.

Fact file

◆ Ice on rivers and lakes is made of millions of frozen **crystals**. The crystals join together to make the ice look smooth.

◆ When it is really cold, the sea can **freeze**. Almost 300 years ago the King of Sweden led his army across the frozen sea to attack Denmark. Unfortunately the ice melted before they reached the other side.

Glossary

black ice thin layer of clear ice – it looks black because the road can be seen through it

continent huge mass of land that has many different countries on it

crops plants grown for food

crystals small shapes of frozen water

expands gets bigger

fleece furry material

freeze change into ice or a solid

invisible cannot be seen

mass amount of something

North and South Poles end points of a line around which the Earth spins. The North and South Poles are very cold.

shelter safe, warm place

surrounded all around, everywhere

thaws melts

tilt moves slightly to one side

vehicles forms of transport. Cars, buses and trucks are all vehicles.

Index